Mel Bay Presents Frequently

M000163590

FAQ

CLASSIC GUITAR CARE AND SETUP
By John LeVan

1 2 3 4 5 6 7 8 9 0

Visit us on the Web at www.melbay.com — E-mail us at email@melbay.com

Foreword

Some years back, while walking through my factory, I was introduced to a young man by my then service manager at Taylor Guitars, Terry Myers. "Bob," he said, "this is John LeVan, the guy I've told you about who's got a repair shop going up in Auburn." "Auburn?" I thought, "What kind of business can a guy do in repairs up in Auburn?"

Auburn is a little wooded town just north of Sacramento, California, and among my favorite spots, actually. The year was 1994 and John was determined to become one of our very first authorized service centers. Terry has since moved to other duties at Taylor Guitars, but at the time he was envisioning repairmen across the country that had the talent to work on our guitars the way we would; fast, efficient, and above all, able to diagnose the true problem with the guitar. Terry worked hard on that goal, but he needed raw talent and a good attitude from the applicants in order to accomplish the task.

So here was John LeVan, spending his time in our repair shop learning our guitars, our methods, our diagnosing procedures; he was learning to have our eyes.

Well, he went home to Auburn, and it came to pass that he grew tremendously in knowledge and eventually relocated to Nashville. This was music to our ears because we now had a man in place in Music City, USA to take care of the many, many Taylor owners there. Nashville is a place with probably the highest population of professionals who use our guitars. John established himself there as an expert guitar repairman who could give great service to people who needed it, both the players and us at Taylor. Our relationship with John has been a joy.

We all know the idea of any category being divided into good, better, and best. I see a lot of people who want to do guitar repairs and be an expert at it. But I don't see people who are hungry for knowledge and experience on how to really be an expert, and are willing to put in the time necessary and check their ego at the door in order to learn. This expertise I'm referring to starts with the skill of looking at a guitar and deciding what the problem is. (You have no idea how many times a neck is re-fretted when what the guitar actually needs is to be humidified!) After that, it moves on to the expertise of how to effectively accomplish the repair, all in the given time allotted, and then returning that guitar to its owner at the promised time.

John LeVan has done more than gather knowledge, he has amassed it. When I read this book I see John's habits on the page - look at the guitar, assess the problem, clean the workbench and gather the right tools, wash your hands, put on a smile, and get it done properly, with the least effort.

It's amazing that after less than a lifetime of guitar repair John can be so organized and energized to put it all in the form of a book like this, thus passing on the information to others. Please take a good look and learn some things from a person who is an expert learner himself.

Bob Taylor

Dedication

I dedicate this book to my wife Wendy and my two daughters, Sarah and Sophia, who every day remind me that life is precious, fragile and miraculous.

Acknowledgments

I would like to thank all of the people who have encouraged, supported and apprenticed me in the craft of luthrie. Special thanks to my Lord Jesus Christ for creating me and giving me a wife that will tolerate me. To my wife, Wendy, for putting up with me for all of these years. Lt. Col. John Nargoso Bilson, for making a man out of me. Brad Shreve, the first person to teach me anything about guitar repair. Karl (with a 'K') Mischler, for teaching me how to play the guitar. Michael Lewis, for including me in the creation of the Sacramento Valley Luthiers Guild. Bob Taylor and Terry Myers, for believing in me enough to let me study at the Taylor® Guitar Factory and showing me how a real repair shop is run, and for the great photographs and diagrams. Tom Anderson®, for affording me the opportunity to learn an excellent technique of fretwork, and opening my eyes to a new temperament. Everyone at Gruhn® Guitars, for all of their support and friendship, especially Ben Burgett and Andy Jellison for teaching me cutting-edge repair techniques. Seymour Duncan®, thanks for all the great diagrams, support and products. Lloyd Baggs from L.R. Baggs®, the excellent pictures, product and information for the book. Jay Hostetler from Stewart-MacDonald® for providing us with great tools. Skip Anderson, for invaluable advice. Finally, my heartfelt thanks to all of the good people who have trusted me with their instruments. Without all of you, I'd probably still be working in a gas station.

Table of Contents

Chapter 9: Other Training Resources 74

Guitar Repair and Maintenance Kit

It's important to use the correct tool for the job. Likewise it is important to buy quality tools that will last. The quality of your tools is reflected in your work, and your work is your calling card. Every guitar you work on is like a résumé, so be sure to do your best. Below is a list of tools and materials recommended to perform the tasks outlined in this book. Here is what you need to get started:

6-Piece Screwdriver Set	**Vacuum (with brush attachment)**
6-Piece Miniature Needle File Set	**Toothbrush**
Precision Scale (Rule)	**Nut Drivers**
14-Piece Hex Key Set	**X-Acto Knives**
10-Piece Nut File Set	**Magnifying Lamp**
String Winder	**Drill and Bits**
Cordless Drill	**Guitar Tuner**
Wire Cutters	**Humidifier**
Polish Cloth	**Safety Glasses**
Straight Edge	

The six-piece screwdriver set should include a small, medium and large tip Phillips head screwdriver, and a small, medium and large tip flathead screwdriver.

FIGURE 1.1 Here are the tools you will need to complete the projects in this book. (Photo by John LeVan)

FIGURE 1.2 The six-piece miniature needle file set should be single-cut, Swiss, and made of carbide steel. (Photo by John LeVan)

Your file set should include:

1. Round File
2. Flat File
3. Square File
4. Half-Round File
5. Three-Cornered File
6. Flat Triangular File

These files will be used to carve and intonate a bridge saddle, file fret ends, spot level a fret, clean out and cut the string slots in the string nut.

FIGURE 1.3A The precision scale rule is a small, six-inch, metal ruler that measures from 1/64" on up. This is important because many of the measurements in this book are in 1/64" and 1/32". Be sure that your scale has good contrast to make it easier to read. (Photo by John LeVan)

FIGURE 1.3 B, An Action Gauge® (sold by Stewart MacDonald®) is an excellent tool for measuring the action on a guitar. (Photo by John LeVan)

10

FIGURE 1.4 The 10-piece nut file set is critical to carving a string nut as well as the final steps to a setup. You'll need these sizes; .010, .012, .016, .022, .026, .032, .036, .040, .046, .052. The above listed files are two-sided, made of carbide steel and are absolutely necessary. (Photo by John LeVan)

FIGURE 1.5 There are many types of string winders on the market. Varying from $.99 to $29, this is one tool that will save you a lot of time and energy. I prefer the type that sets into a cordless drill, thus speeding up the restringing process and minimizing fatigue and the risk of developing tendonitis. (Photo by John LeVan)

When choosing a cordless drill, I recommend a rechargeable model with a pistol grip, torque clutch, reverse capability, and at least 500 rpm. As for wire cutters, a six-inch pair of angled pliers works well. The only polish cloth I use in my shop is a 100% cotton, Birdseye Weave Cloth Diaper.

FIGURE 1.6 Straight edges are essential for sighting a neck and checking the frets to see if they are level. There are several sizes and types that I recommend including 1", 4", 6", 12", 24" to 36" and even one that is notched out where the frets are to check that fretboard is true (straight with the proper radius). (Photo by John LeVan)

FIGURE 1.7 A vacuum with a round brush attachment will help you clean up metal filings and dust when working on a guitar. I prefer a small shop vac, however most uprights have all the attachments you need, *just don't tell your spouse I said to use it.* (Photo by John LeVan)

A medium to hard bristle toothbrush is perfect for scrubbing while applying lemon oil to your fret board. *Remember - it's not nice to use someone else's toothbrush without asking first!*

Miscellaneous:

There are nine nut driver sizes that will be the most useful. 1/4", 5/16", 9/32", 11/32", 7/16", 1/2", 9/16", 6mm, 10mm are used for everything from adjusting a trussrod to tightening an endpin jack. X-Acto® knife sets are very handy around the shop. They come with several types of replacement blades and handles. These are used for scoring, cleaning glue out of a fret slot, etc. Magnifying lamps help you see detail that you normally can't see with the naked eye. Warning - this can be a very humbling experience. An electric drill and bits are needed when boring out the end block to install an endpin jack, installing an acoustic guitar pickup and all those other projects that require more torque than what your cordless drill has. You will need bits in all standard (not metric) sizes from 1/16" to 1/8". You may also want a tapered ream for boring to install an endpin jack.

Tuners:

FIGURE 1.8 There are many choices when it comes to choosing a guitar tuner. Most tuners are really not accurate enough to intonate a guitar properly. Our shop tuner is accurate to +\- 1/100 of one cent, where one note = 100 cent. Most tuners are +/- three to five cent. I recommend a tuner that is at least +/- one cent for intonating a guitar. Most guitar tuners publish their accuracy ratings in their brochures. (Photos by John LeVan)

FIGURE 1.9 Humidifiers are one of the least expensive ways to prevent damage to a guitar. Our shop has warm mist humidifiers in the room as well as some you install inside your guitar during transport and storage. Humidity will be covered in detail in Chapter 2. (Photo by John LeVan)

Always wear your safety glasses. Safety first, convenience second!

Materials:

Here is a list of the most common materials that will be needed for general guitar repair and maintenance.

- Wood Glue (Tightbond® I and Tightbond® II, RBC® Epoxy)
- Super Glue®, Thick and Thin (Jet® or Zap® brand)
- Super Glue® Accelerator
- Super Glue® Solvent
- 1,500 Grit Self-Adhesive Sandpaper
- 220 Grit Self-Adhesive Sandpaper
- 0000 Steel Wool
- Masking Tape
- Guitar Polish
- Suction Cup
- Lemon Oil
- Q-Tips®

FIGURE 1.10 Here are the materials and supplies needed to complete the repairs in this book. (Photo by John LeVan)

Wood glue is needed for structural repairs. Tightbond® I is great for neck resets and bridge plate repairs. Tightbond® II is better for broken headstocks, body cracks and bridge re-glues. RBC® Epoxy is good for crack repairs that require color matching. It can be mixed with fresco powder to match the paint or lacquer color of the guitar you're repairing. Super Glue® (cyanoacrylite), is manufactured by several companies. Zap® and Jet® are two that have given me great results. They come in a wide range of viscosities, from water thin to the thickness of molasses. We use the ultra thin, thin and thick the most. This type of glue works great for securing a string nut, loose frets and minor touch up on acrylic and polyurethane finishes. Be sure to also have super Glue® accelerator (to speed up drying time) and Super Glue® solvent (in case you glue your finger to your chin).

Self-adhesive sandpaper is always a must for any repair shop, with 1,500 grit being best for polishing (burnishing) frets and polishing bone string nuts and saddles. It also comes in handy for sanding out finish scratches. Use 220-grit sandpaper for fret leveling and carving string nuts and bridge saddles. I recommend 0000 steel wool to do a final polish on the frets as well as to clean the fretboard. Never use anything more coarse on a guitar, it could damage the frets. Low-tack 3" masking tape will be useful to tape off pickups while cleaning. Commercial guitar polishes will work fine on most finishes; just don't use any polish on satin finishes as it will make them look inconsistent and hazy. Lemon oil is the best substance to condition a rosewood or ebony fretboard. It is highly recommended to condition and clean your guitar regularly. Q-Tips® are an absolute necessity whenever you use glue of any type. They are also handy for cleaning hard to reach places like under a bridge saddle or between your toes. There are several brands available and most are adequate.

Sources:

- LeVan's Guitar Services (615) 251-8884 • www.guitarservices.com
- Luthier's Mercantile® (800) 477-4437 • www.lmii.com
- Stewart-MacDonald® (800) 848-2273 • www.stewmac.com
- All Parts® (800) 327-8942 • www.allparts.com

Hygiene

The key to preventing corrosion, cracking and poor guitar hygiene is to clean and condition your guitar every time you change your strings.

One of the most overlooked parts of owning a guitar is cleaning and conditioning it regularly. Why is this so important? Because the more you play your guitar the more dirt, sweat and oils build up on it. As a result, your strings, frets and bridge receive the brunt of the damage. The acid in sweat and the oils from your fingers corrodes the strings causing them to lose their bright tone. Likewise, sweat and oils condense on the frets causing the wood around them to deteriorate. If left unconditioned, the fretboard and bridge are likely to crack.

So how do you prevent these filthy afflictions from ravaging your guitar? It all starts with good hygiene.

The first step to good guitar hygiene is player cleanliness.

- Wash your hands before you play.
- Wipe your strings with a clean dry cloth after playing.
- Make your *friends* wash their hands before you let them play *your* guitar.
- Good hygiene is good guitar care!

It also helps to store your guitar in its case, and occasionally vacuum the case.

Materials Needed:

- 0000 Steel Wool (only 0000, never anything more coarse)
- Vacuum (with brush attachment)
- Toothbrush
- Paper Towels
- Lemon Oil
- Guitar Polish

Cleaning

There are a few fundamental steps to cleaning your guitar. The first step is to remove the strings - *YES ALL OF THEM*. It does not damage the guitar to remove all strings at one time. Next, you need to scrub the fretboard with 0000 steel wool in the direction of the grain of the wood. This will clean the dirt and grime off of your fretboard as well as polish the frets. **DO NOT USE 0, 00 or 000 steel wool,** *only* *0000.* If your guitar has a maple or blond fretboard, then you'll need to either cover the wood with masking tape (only exposing the metal frets) or skip using the steel wool. The fine grit 0000 steel wool won't damage the frets or fretboard. Avoid getting it on the finish.

Scrubbing the Fretboard

Scrubbing the fretboard will remove dirt, dead skin cells and other things that collect on your fretboard. You should do this every time you change your strings. The steps are as follows:

- Scrub the frets using the 0000 steel wool "with the grain" of the wood; 99.99 percent of the time "with the grain" means the length of the neck.

FIGURE 2.1 Scrub the fretboard with the grain, not against the grain. (Photo by John LeVan)

- After the fretboard is clean and the frets are polished, use a vacuum to remove all of the steel wool from the guitar. Make sure you vacuum the entire guitar and around the bench too.

Conditioning

Conditioning your guitar is easy. All you need is a toothbrush, lemon oil and paper towels.

- Just dip your toothbrush into the lemon oil and then scrub the fretboard. Make sure that you cover the entire fretboard. A great thing about lemon oil is that you can't overoil your fretboard, it will only absorb what it needs.

- After the lemon oil settles into the wood for a few minutes, simply wipe off the excess with a dry paper towel.

FIGURE 2.2 Most toothbrushes won't damage the fretboard. Don't be afraid of scrubbing it into the wood. (Photo by John LeVan)

Now is a good time to clean the rest of the body using a damp paper towel and a few drops of lemon oil. This process will make your guitar look and perform at its best.

Restringing

After thoroughly cleaning and conditioning your guitar, you are ready to restring it. Depending upon what kind of guitar you have (classical, electric, acoustic, bass, etc) there are several techniques that can be applied. For a classical or nylon-string guitar, the strings are tied on using a looping method.

Tools Needed:

- String Winder (manual or electric)
- String Cutters (end cutters, dykes, nippers)
- Guitar Tuner
- Patience

FIGURE 2.3 Electric or manual, a good string winder is essential to restringing a guitar. Likewise, a 6" pair of end cutters and an accurate guitar tuner are a must. (Photo by John LeVan)

Note: Classical or nylon-string guitars are the most challenging to restring.

FIGURE 2.4A,B,C,D,E Pull the string through the bridge, then over the top of the bridge, under and around itself (counterclockwise). Then, wrap the string under itself with the final wrap on the back edge of the bridge. (Photos by John LeVan)

Restringing a Classical Guitar

Make sure that you do not overwind the strings (wrap the string too many times around the roller). This can cause a world of tuning problems. Underwinding the string is just as bad. Following the above diagram, tie the strings using the looping method. The two treble strings, (B and E) are each looped through the bridge twice. This technique will minimize all the extra stretching that the string will incur. Classical strings stretch for several days before they settle into tune. It's also a good idea to singe the ends of the treble strings with a lighter before you tie them on. This prevents any additional string slippage.

Next, tie the strings onto the tuning key roller. This is where it gets a little more complex. But don't worry, you'll catch on once you've done a few more restrings. Note that the two E string windings are wound in opposite directions towards the outside, and the rest of the strings are wound towards each other. This is because of the design of the headstock. Stretch! Slowly stretch the strings. After you stretch the strings, tune, tune, and retune.

FIGURE 2.5A,B,C,D,E Pull the string through the tuning key roller, then around the back of the roller, under and around itself (clockwise), then wrap the string under itself and give a firm tug. (Photos by John LeVan)

FIGURE 2.6 Acoustic guitar bridges are made from ebony, ivory, rosewood, micarda, and even plastic. The bridge saddle can be made from plastic, bone, ivory, graphite, brass, micarda or wood. Bone and ivory tend to give the most volume and dynamic range. (Photo by John LeVan)

The bridge assembly includes

- Bridge
- Bridge Saddle
- Bridge Plate

Transporting and Storage

When transporting and storing your guitar it's important to do so in a consistent environment. **When shipping a guitar,**

- Slightly de-tune the strings just in case it is jarred while in transit. A sudden impact can cause structural damage when the guitar is under tension.

- Install a fretguard to prevent the strings from damaging the frets if the guitar is dropped or jarred. A piece of cardboard or file folder will work.

- Secure your guitar in a quality ATA-certified guitar case and be sure that it doesn't have any wiggle room. *A snug case makes for a safer guitar.*

- Place all peripheral equipment in either the storage compartment of the case or in a separate bag. Do not leave anything in the case that can slide, fall or bounce on or into your guitar.

Detuning the strings (a few turns on each key) will help prevent extra tension on the guitar. This is especially important for acoustic guitars.

FIGURE 2.7 Fretguards will prevent any damage to your frets from an impact on the guitar case. The fret guard slides between the frets and the strings, protecting the frets from the strings cutting into them during an impact. (Photo by John LeVan)

ATA®-certified cases are approved for air travel. They are generally made from plywood, metal or ABS® plastic. Even with an ATA® certified case, it is important that the guitar does not move freely within the case. If it does move, I recommend using a towel or foam rubber to secure the guitar within the case.

Always store peripheral items such as a tuner, capo and string cutters, etc. in the middle compartment of the case. No good will come of a pair of string cutters bouncing off your guitar while in transit.

If you must store your guitar for any length of time, it needs to be in a consistent environment. That means the temperature and humidity should not fluctuate much more than 10 degrees and 10 percent humidity. A temperature of 70-80 degrees Fahrenheit is relatively safe, and 40 - 50 percent humidity is best. Again, it's a good idea to detune your guitar a whole step down from standard pitch.

Humidity and Temperature

Humidity is the amount of moisture in the air. Too much or too little humidity can make you guitar sound, play and look very bad. Around 40-50 percent humidity is ideal for a guitar. If a guitar is left in an environment that is too hot or too cold, (like the trunk of a car on a hot day) the result can be devastating. It only takes a few hours of heat to melt the glue that holds your guitar together. Acoustic instruments are affected more than electric guitars because they are made from thinner pieces of wood and are under more stress and tension. All instruments, however, need a consistent environment. Here is a list of problems that occur as a result of extremely low humidity:

- Structural Cracks (bridge, neck, top, back, sides)
- Sharp Fret Ends (caused by the fretboard shrinking)
- Warped Neck
- Loose Braces
- Glue Failure
- Cracked Finish (finish checking)
- String Rattle
- Intonation and Tuning Problems

FIGURE 2.8 This guitar was badly damaged by low humidity. Notice the sunken top, excessively forebowed neck, and the high neck angle. There is usually other hidden damage inside the guitar that requires extensive repairs. (Illustration provided by the Taylor Guitar® Company)

How to Gauge Humidity

There are several products on the market to help you discern the humidity level in your environment. I recommend a digital one that measures both temperature and humidity. Most hardware stores as well as home improvement stores stock them; they retail from $14 to $30. Regardless of which one you choose, consider it to be a very cheap insurance policy for your guitar.

FIGURE 2.9 Most hygrometers will show both the temperature and humidity. (Photo provided by J. D'Addario & Co®.)

How to Control Humidity

There are two types of humidifiers that I recommend depending upon where and how your guitar is stored. If your guitar is outside of the case, than I recommend a warm-mist room humidifier. Used with your hygrometer (humidity gauge), this method is quite efficient. If your guitar is kept inside the case, I recommend either the "Damp-it®" or the "Planet Waves®" humidifier. Either of these humidifiers can be found in most music stores for between $12 and $16. Even with an in-case humidifier, it is still important to use a hygrometer to measure the humidity wherever your guitar is stored.

FIGURE 2.10 Here are a few of the different types of guitar humidifiers available on the market. (Photo by John LeVan)

Summary

To prolong the life of your guitar, here is what you need to remember:

1. **Hygiene** (wash up before you play, wipe down the strings when finished playing)

2. **Clean and condition your guitar** (0000 steel wool, lemon oil and guitar polish)

3. **Restring** (strings should last about 20 to 30 playing hours if you keep them clean)

4. **Humidity and temperature** (keep you guitar in a consistent environment)

This guide will help prevent premature wear and tear on your guitar and hopefully reduce costly visits to the repair shop.

Adjusting the Neck

This is the first step in a setup. It is a critical part of the entire process because, if it is done incorrectly, you will have to repeat the following steps in the setup procedure. Chapters 3-6 outline the procedure for doing a setup. Not all classical guitars have a trussrod. If your guitar does not have a trussrod, you may skip this chapter.

List of Components

See figure 3.1

The neck has several important components such as:

1. Headstock (can be a multitude of shapes and sizes)

2. Tuning Keys (various colors and styles)

3. Trussrod Cover (not found on all guitars)

4. Trussrod Nut (this can be found at either end of the neck in different guitars)

5. String Nut (made of bone, metal, ivory, wood or plastic)

6. Fretboard (usually made of ebony or rosewood, maple, micarda or graphite)

7. Frets (nickel, silver and zinc alloy)

8. Trussrod (single-action, double-action or K-bar)

9. Trussrod anchor (can be found at either end of the neck in different guitars)

10. Neck Slab (maple, rosewood, graphite or mahogany)

11. Heel (where the neck attaches to the body)

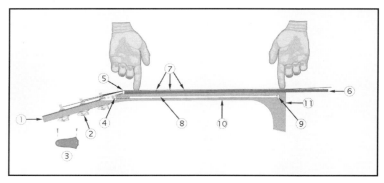

FIGURE 3.1 Here are the components of a guitar neck listed on page 29. (Illustration provided by the Taylor Guitar® Company.)

An important aspect of guitar repair is the way in which you record measurements. The measurements you record will help you see the corrections you make as you work on your instrument. Throughout this book we will be recording many different measurements in order to compare the guitar before and after it has been setup. Here are a few foolproof techniques for sighting and adjusting the neck.

To measure the amount of relief (bow) in a neck

1. Tune the guitar to whatever pitch the player will be using

2. Place a capo on top of the first fret over the strings

3. Hold the guitar in playing position

4. Press down low E at the last fret

5. Use your precision scale (ruler) or Stewart-MacDonald® Action Gauge® to measure the distance from the top of the frets to the bottom of the low E string at the middle of the neck

6. Record the largest distance between the frets and string

The first step in setting up any guitar is adjusting the neck. This step is critical because if the neck has too much forebow and you adjust the action at the nut, you will need to replace the nut after you readjust the neck properly. The same is probable if you adjust the action at the bridge (on an acoustic guitar) before adjusting the neck. Unnecessary replacement of parts should be avoided. **The goal is to be accurate, efficient and effective.**

Repeating steps will just waste time and energy. Before sighting the neck, make sure that the guitar is tuned to "concert pitch" (A-440) or whatever tuning the player will be using. Next, sight the neck to check for either a backbow (convex) or a forebow (concave).

There are three basic methods of sighting a neck.

1. Visually looking down the neck from the headstock.
2. Holding down the low E string at the 1st and last fret.
3. Setting a straight edge on top of the fingerboard.

Method No. 1 is great if you just want to "eyeball" the neck. However, it isn't very accurate for taking measurements. This technique will help you make a quick judgment as to whether the neck is fore-bowed or back-bowed.

FIGURE 3.2 Holding the neck at the headstock, look down the fretboard to determine if the neck is fore-bowed or back-bowed. (Photo by John LeVan)

Method No. 2 is the easiest way to record an accurate measurement as long as the low E string is in good condition. *If it is bent or dented, your measurement will be inaccurate.* By placing a capo at the first fret and holding the low E string down at the last fret, you can determine just how much forebow a neck has. If the neck is back-bowed, then you will not be able to record any measurements using this method.

FIGURE 3.3A Note that the capo must be on top of the first fret, not in front of or behind it. (Photo by John LeVan)

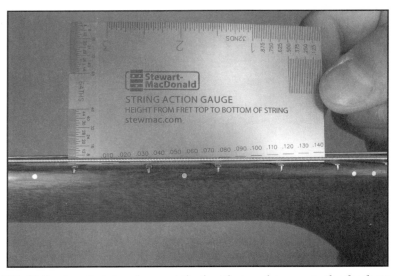

3.3B Hold the low E string down at the last fret and measure the farthest distance between the top of the fret to the bottom of the low E string. (Photo by John LeVan)

Method No. 3 is also a good technique to use when measuring the amount of relief in a neck. Even if the neck is *back-bowed* you can still measure the amount of backbow by holding the straight edge on top of the frets and measuring the distance between the bottom of the straight edge and the *top of the first (or 14th) fret.* The greater distance should be recorded. If the neck has a *forebow,* then hold the straight edge on top of the frets and measure the distance from the bottom of the straight edge to the *top the frets in the middle of the neck.*

FIGURE 3.4 Method No. 3 is the same concept as method No. 2, however you are substituting the low E string with the straight edge. When using method No. 3, be sure to place the straight edge between the D and G strings on top of the frets. As always, record the greatest distance between the top of the frets and the bottom of the straight edge. (Photo by John LeVan)

The Trussrod.

Inside the neck is a trussrod. To adjust the neck, tighten or loosen the trussrod. By tightening the trussrod you can force it to straighten or even backbow. When you loosen the trussrod, it releases the pressure and forebows or becomes concave. Turning the trussrod clockwise will tighten it and counter-clockwise will loosen it. If the neck is back bowed, then loosen the rod; If the neck is fore-bowed, then tighten the rod. **[When working on a vintage or old guitar you should always loosen the strings before tightening the trussrod].** If you don't you risk stripping the rod and that's an expensive repair! **When in doubt, consult with a qualified luthier.**

FIGURE 3.5A Here is a diagram of a trussrod, trussrod nut, and anchor. (Illustration provided by the Taylor Guitar® Company.)

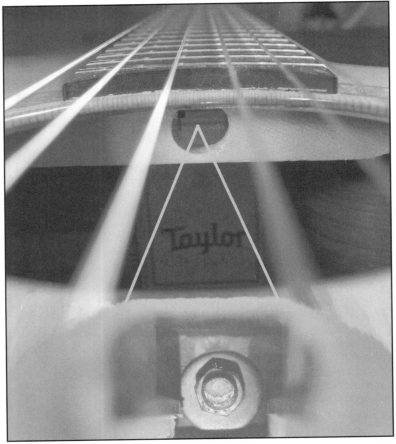

FIGURE 3.5B This is a close-up view of where the trussrod is located on a Taylor® Brand Classical Guitar. (Photo by John LeVan)

FIGURE 3.6A Here is a neck with too much forebow or too much relief in it. The trussrod needs to be tightened from the sound hole by turning it clockwise. (Photo by John LeVan)

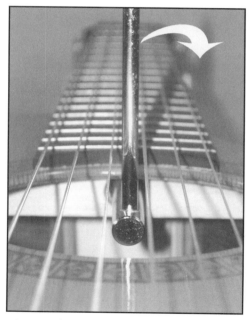

FIGURE 3.6B Here is a neck with too much forebow or too much relief in it. The trussrod needs to be tightened from the sound hole by turning it clockwise. (Photo by John LeVan)

FIGURE 3.7 Here is a correctly adjusted neck. (Photo by John LeVan)

FIGURE 3.8A Here is a neck that is convex or back-bowed. The trussrod needs to be loosened from the sound hole by turning it counter-clockwise. (Photo by John LeVan)

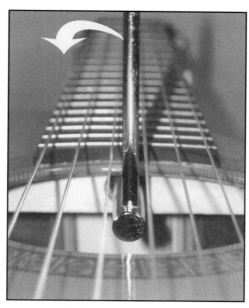

FIGURE 3.8B Here is a neck that is convex or back-bowed. The trussrod needs to be loosened from the sound hole by turning it counter-clockwise. (Photo by John LeVan)

Most trussrod adjustments require a hex key, screwdriver or a nut driver (socket wrench). See illustrations above. There should be a slight amount of fore-bow in the neck, (approximately .010" to .015") dependent upon the instrument and condition of the neck. If the player wants fast and low action, .010" of relief is plenty. If the player uses a capo or is heavy-handed, then .015" or more is recommended.

We will discuss neck adjustments in this book in depth. *The object of the exercise is to adjust the guitar to the player.* Knowing the style and technique of the player is critical to properly adjusting the guitar. Everyone has his or her own style and technique, that's why it's important to match the setup to the player.

There are two types of trussrods, adjustable and non-adjustable. Non-adjustable are also called K-bars or steel-reinforced rods. Adjustable trussrods come in two varieties, single and double action.

Single-action trussrods only force the neck in one direction. As you tighten a single-action trussrod, it forced it to straighten or backbow the neck. When you loosen the rod it releases the pressure. These are common in most guitars. A common dilemma is when you have a neck that is backbowed even after you have completely loosened the trussrod. To correct this you either have to replace the trussrod or plane and re-fret the neck. Both repairs are expensive and require an experienced luthier.

Single-Action Trussrod

FIGURE 3.9 Single action trussrods are common in most modern guitars. This type of trussrod will only force the neck in one direction. (Illustration by John LeVan)

Double-action trussrods force the neck in both directions. If the trussrod is loose and the neck is still backbowed, then keep turning it until it forces the neck in the other direction. These trussrods are more stable and are usually found in finer guitars and basses.

Double-Action Trussrod

FIGURE 3.10 Double-action trussrods will force the neck in two directions. (Illustration by John LeVan)

Troubleshooting

As I mentioned earlier, trussrod repairs are difficult and expensive. In many cases it is more cost effective to buy a new neck than it is to repair a broken trussrod. There are several things that can go wrong with a trussrod. They can freeze or rust, break, strip and cause the neck and fretboard to separate. Here are a few tips to identify a damaged trussrod:

- It spins freely when tightening
- It will not turn in either direction
- Rattles inside the neck when you play
- Has been run over by a car!

Occasionally, the only damage is the trussrod nut has stripped. If this is the case, then simply replace it and your back in business. A new trussrod nut is about $2. Whatever the case may be, if you are unsure, ask a professional. There is no substitute for experience, and nothing builds confidence like the experiences you will gain with time.

If the trussrod will not tighten, back off the trussrod nut and check to see if either the nut or rod is stripped. If the nut is stripped, replace it. If the rod is stripped, take it to a qualified luthier.

Adjusting the Action at the Bridge

Adjusting the action at the bridge is step two in the setup process. We adjust the string height at the bridge in order to make it easier to play the higher notes on the neck of the guitar. In step one we adjusted the neck, in step two we'll adjust the height of the bridge.

Components

- Classic Guitar Bridge

FIGURE 4.1 Classic guitar bridges come in many sizes and shapes, but generally contain the same components: bridge saddle, saddle slot, holes (for the strings) and the bridge base. (Photo by John LeVan)

The player's style is the deciding factor on an absolute height to follow. The strings should consistently graduate at least 1/64" from high E to low E, with the high E closest to the frets. This will compensate for the difference in thickness in the strings. If every string were the same height, either the treble strings would be too high or the bass strings would tend to rattle.

Adjusting the action at the bridge can be done several ways depending upon the instrument. An electric guitar can be corrected by simply adjusting a thumb-wheel or an Allen-screw. An acoustic or classical guitar is generally adjusted by sanding the bottom of the bridge saddle. One of the most important elements of a good setup is adjusting the guitar for the player's particular style. If the player is heavy-handed, the action (or distance of the strings to the frets) needs to be higher; if the player has a light touch then the action can be lower. If the action is too high, then the guitar can be difficult to play and can cause intonation problems. If too low, it can cause string rattle and dead spots on the string.

Measuring the Action at the Bridge

1. I recommend a well-machined scale (ruler) or Action Gauge® with good contrast that will measure to 1/64".

2. Place a capo over the strings on top of the first fret.

3. Measure the distance from the top of the 12th fret to the bottom of each string.

4. Record your measurements.

FIGURE 4.2 A good scale (rule) to use is one that is 1/4" x up to 6", with sharp contrast which makes it easy to read. The Stewart-MacDonald® Action Gauge® is an excellent tool. (Photo by John LeVan)

FIGURE 4.3 When measuring the action at the 12th fret, make sure your scale is level when you place it on top of the fret. It is also helpful to have a lot of light on the subject so that you can clearly see the measurements. (Photo by John LeVan)

Start with the high E and work your way to the low E. After you record the measurements for each string, adjust the action of each string to the desired height. Keep in mind that you'll need to set the low E string approximately 1/64" higher than the high E string. All the other strings will graduate somewhere in between. The B string will be slightly higher than the high E, the G string will be slightly higher than the B string, etc.

FIGURE 4.4 A gradual increase in the height of each string is the goal. If you raise the action too much, the guitar will be difficult to play. Too little, and it will rattle and buzz. (Photo by John LeVan)

When adjusting the bridge on a classical guitar, remove the saddle from the bridge. Be sure to mark the bottom of the saddle with a mechanical pencil to show the amount of saddle you intend to remove. It is imperative to sand the saddle flush and square on the bottom to ensure a solid fit. This will also prevent any balancing problems if there is an under saddle pickup. The best way I have found to do this is to use a flat surface (like a marble slab or counter top) and self-adhesive sandpaper (220 grit). Sand the saddle away from yourself in one direction. The object of the exercise is to keep consistent pressure on the saddle so that it ends up perfectly flat and square on the bottom. If you fail to keep the saddle perpendicular to the sand-paper, the saddle will be uneven and result in tone loss and uneven string balance. Check the saddle periodically to be sure that you don't remove too much at a time. As with other types of guitars, you should leave a height difference of about 1/64" from low E to high E. Keep in mind that if the saddle is not compensated (intonated), then you may need to leave it about 1/64" taller so it doesn't end up too low after you set the intonation. Classical guitars have nylon strings and are played with a broad dynamic range. As a result, the action needs to be higher than the average acoustic, these guitars are usually fingerpicked using fingernails instead of guitar picks.

FIGURE 4.5 Carefully mark the bottom of the saddle. A mechanical pencil works great. I recommend marking both sides of the saddle so you can see if you are sanding it flat of if you are tilting to one side or the other. (Photo by John LeVan)

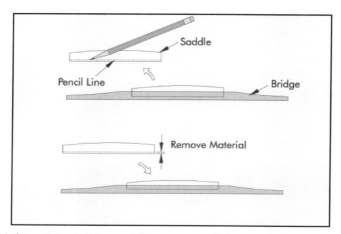

FIGURE 4.6 Sand the bridge saddle square and flat on the bottom. If you tilt it while sanding, the saddle won't be flush to the saddle slot. This can be a problem if the guitar has an under-saddle pickup. (Illustration provided by the Taylor Guitar® Company)

FIGURE 4.7 Keep the action high enough to accomodate the player's style of play. (Photo by John LeVan)

Adjusting the Action at the Nut

Adjusting the action at the nut is step three of a setup. This is a very important part of the setup because if the action is too high at the nut, the guitar will be difficult to play and will not play in tune.

So far we have done step one (adjusting the neck) and step two (adjusting the action at the bridge); now we'll do step three (adjusting the action at the nut).

List of Components

String Nut

- String Slots
- String Angles
- Slot Width
- String Spacing
- Precision Scale/Rule

FIGURE 5.1 Here is a photo of the string nut. (Illustration by John LeVan)

Tools Needed:

- Nut Files
- Scale (Miniature Metal Ruler)
- Action Gauge® by Stewart-MacDonald®

FIGURE 5.2A,B Nut files and a scale are essential to doing this procedure correctly. Make sure to choose the correct nut files for the guitar you are working on, and in particular, for the gauge of strings being used on it. (Photos by John LeVan)

A proven way to adjust the string height at the nut is to use a set of nut files. I recommend 7 different sizes:

• .022   • .026

• .032   • .036

• .040   • .046

• .052

Angles, Width and Spacing

It is critically important to cut the slot at the correct angle, width and spacing. The *angle* of the slot should match the angle of the string from the front of the nut to the tuning key roller. If the slot angle is incorrect, then the string will either rattle or not intonate properly. If the string slot is not cut to the proper width, then it can cause tuning problems, string breakage and string rattle. The *width* of the slot is equally important. When the slot is too narrow the string will bind in the slot and can break as well as cause tuning problems. If the slot is cut too wide, the string will rattle and buzz when played in the open position. String *spacing* is the distance from one string to another. If there is a greater space between the B and G string than between the A and low E string, then the spacing is incorrect. This can make the guitar difficult to play. Each string should be the same distance from the next. Measuring from the outside edge of the strings, all the strings should be the same distance from each other.

FIGURE 5.3 Be sure to cut the string slot at the same angle as the string from the face of the nut to the crest of the tuning roller. (Photo by John LeVan)

47

Never cut the slot more that 2/1000" wider than the diameter of the string. Equally as important is to avoid cutting the slot too narrow.

**FIGURE 5.4 To measure the action at the nut, place the Action Guage®
on top of the 1st fret. Record the distance from the top of the fret to the
bottom of each string. (Photo by John LeVan)**

Proper Adjustments

All proper adjustments begin with accurate measurements.

To measure action at the nut, tune the guitar to pitch and place your rule on top of the first fret at the high E string. Record the distance from the top of the fret to the bottom of the string. Generally you need about 1/64" or 15/1000" distance from the top of the fret to the bottom of the string for the high E string. For the low E string double the distance. *Keep in mind that the actual height will ultimately be determined by the player's style. If the player is heavy-handed, you need to add about .010" of height.* **The low E should be slightly higher than the high E by at least 1/64".** The rest of the strings should be an ascending balance between the two E strings. In other words, the B string will be slightly higher than the high E string, the G will be slightly higher than the B string, etc. Because classical strings have less tension than steel strings, they tend to rattle and buzz more when played. It is also common for classical players to play more dynamically and aggressively than steel-string players. **It may take a while to train your eye to see such small detail, but like all skills, practice makes perfect. This is the same formula used in Chapter 4 on adjusting the action at the bridge.**

Replacement vs. Repair

There are times when you just need a quick fix, and there are times when you need a permanent repair. A quick fix is acceptable when you're on the road or don't have the time and resources for a permanent repair. Filling the nut is a quick fix and a temporary repair. You should replace the nut as soon as possible if it's worn or cut too low. Below are some common problems and some quick fixes and permanent solutions.

When the string slot is cut too low. The strings will rattle on the open notes in what is often called the *sitar effect.* There are two ways to fix this problem.

1. Fill the string slot with a material that is the same as what the nut is made of

2. Replace the nut

If you don't have the resources to replace the nut, then the next best thing is to fill the slot and re-cut it. Again, this is only a temporary fix until you can replace it.

Filling the Nut Slot

*   Clean out the slot removing any dirt, graphite or glue

*   Then fill slot with either bone or plastic dust [whatever material the nut is made of]

*   Add a drop of Super Glue® to seal and bond the dust into the slot

*   Spray Super Glue® Accelerator onto slot (glue will dry immediately)

*   Re-cut the slot to the correct depth

FIGURE 5.5 Clean out the slot using a nut file. You may want to use a file that is slightly larger than the slot for this. (Photo by John LeVan)

FIGURE 5.6 Loosely pack the slot with a like material to the nut. If the nut is bone, use bone. (Photo by John LeVan)

FIGURE 5.7A,B Apply one drop of thin Super Glue® to the slot. Always have a Q-Tip® in your hand when working with Super Glue®. Use the Q-Tip® to absorb any excess glue before it can drip onto the finish. (Photos by John LeVan)

Spray a little bit of Super Glue® accelerator into the slot to speed up the drying process.

FIGURE 5.8 Re-cut the string slot to the correct width, depth and angle. (Photo by John LeVan)

To replace the nut, use a flathead screwdriver and lightly tap the front of the nut with the tip of the screwdriver to break it loose. If this isn't working try a drop of solvent. *Make sure you don't get any of the solvent on the finish of the neck. Solvent can melt the finish of most guitars.* Then clean out the nut slot with a miniature file to remove all the glue before you install the new nut. Be certain that the nut fits snug and flush. Using a drop of thin Super Glue® between the D and the G string to secure it to the end of the fingerboard. Re-cut the string slots to the proper action as per the instructions at the beginning of this chapter.

Setting the Intonation

Setting the intonation is step four of a setup. Without setting the intonation, the guitar will never play even close to being in tune. So far we have completed step one (adjusting the neck), step two (adjusting the action at the bridge), and step three (adjusting the action at the nut); now we'll perform step four-setting the intonation.

Intonation means to be in perfect unison.

The purpose of intonating a guitar is so that it plays in tune both with itself and with other properly intonated instruments. Understanding the fundamentals and variables of intonation is crucial to the performance of any guitar. Even the best guitars are useless if they don't play in tune. Learning to intonate and temper an instrument are skills that you will learn in this chapter. We will define, test and discuss variables and temperaments and how to balance them to the instrument as well as the player.

Tools Needed

While there are many different types of guitar bridges, to intonate a classical guitar you will need only miniature flat files.

FIGURE 6.1 Choose the right tool for the job. The miniature flat file is used to intonate a classical. (Photo by John LeVan)

To adjust the intonation on a classical guitar, the bridge saddle must be carved into the proper position for each string with a miniature flat file. When intonating an acoustic bridge saddle be very careful to carve the angles at the correct pitch. If you carve a saddle too steep, it will result in string breakage, tone loss, volume loss and tuning problems. If you carve it too shallow, the string may rattle over the bridge saddle and the instrument will also lose tone and volume.

FIGURE 6.2 Be sure to carve the saddle to the correct angle with your mini flat file. Take special care not to slip and scratch the bridge or the top. A piece of cardboard or pickguard material is a wise choice to use as a shield or guard during this process. (Photo by John LeVan)

Before you set the intonation, be sure that the following three steps have been completed in order:

1. Adjust the neck

2. Adjust the action at the bridge

3. Adjust the action at the nut

Once the guitar is in tune (using a guitar tuner) and the strings are settled and holding their tune, then check the **12th fret harmonic** against the fretted-note at the 12th fret on each string. Make sure that you read the **attack** of the note not the **drift** when using your tuner. The **attack** is the immediate reaction of the note; **drift** is where the note settles. The goal is to match the harmonic tone with the fretted note. **The harmonic is always true, so that is your constant or control note. The fretted note is always the variable.** It is very important to use an accurate tuner for adjusting the intonation. A Saunderson Accutuner® or a Strobe tuner are the best type on the market at present.

Sharp, Flat and Hopeless? Now that you have established whether the fretted note is either sharp (♯) or flat (♭), it's time to adjust the intonation for each saddle. If the fretted note is sharp (♯) then the saddle for that string needs to be moved away from the neck (back). If the fretted note is flat (♭) then the saddle needs to move towards the neck (forward). **Sharp** (♯) means the string is too **short; flat** (♭) means the string is too **long.**

When intonating a classical gitar the bridge saddle must be carved for each string, as each string has its own angle. If the angle for each string is not carved correctly, it can result in tuning problems, string breakage, tone loss, volume loss, and cracks in the bridge saddle.

Bridge saddles are made from many different materials such as, bone, ivory, Micarta®, Tusq® and plastic. Each material has a specific sound and longevity. Bone and ivory tend to last the longest and sound the best.

Variables and tempering need to be identified and understood in order to control them. A critical variable to intonating is the string nut. If the front of the nut is worn or chipped, it can cause the intonation to be sharp (♯). This is why intonating is the last step in a setup.

Other variables include:

- Worn Frets
- Inaccurate Fret Placement
- Inaccurate Nut Placement
- Inaccurate Bridge Saddle Placement
- Strumming Technique
- Fret Height
- How Hard the Player Presses the Strings

One of the most widely used calculations to determine nut, fret and saddle placement is the *Rule of 18.* The Rule of 18 is rather complicated, however, if the placement of the above listed components are not correct, the guitar will never play in tune. Six out of seven of the above listed variables are correctable, fret placement is not cost effective to correct. However, there are adjustments that can be made to offset this common problem.

Believe it or not, no instrument can play perfectly in tune. Thus, the art of *tempering* was developed. Tempering is the balancing of tones to make an instrument sound more pleasing to the ear. In other words, each string on a guitar is intonated and tuned slightly off pitch in order to make most chords sound in tune. the piano is commonly temper-tuned in order to play in tune with itself. Likewise, a guitar can also be temper-tuned. This practice dates back to the time of Bach when he nearly lost his head because he subverted tradition by temper-tuning his piano.

This completes the setup process. At this point we have completed step one (adjusting the neck), step two (adjusting the action at the bridge), step three (adjusting the action at the nut), and finally, step four (setting the intonation). Your guitar should now play better than ever, and who knows? Maybe someday you'll be on the concert stage!

Top 10 Signs of a Problematic Guitar

Before you purchase an instrument, make sure that you completely inspect it. It is always a good idea to bring along someone who can identify serious problems and defects when you shop for an instrument. Many repair shops offer an "evaluation" or "inspection" for a small fee. It's better to pay $20 or $30 to find a serious problem before you buy, than to spend over $1,000 on an instrument that needs an overhaul.

Classical Guitar

1. Won't play in tune
2. Fret wear
3. Worn string nut
4. Cracked bridge
5. Sharp fret ends
6. Loose braces
7. Won't hold tuning
8. Loose tuning keys
9. Body cracks
10. Bad neck angle

In order for a guitar to intonate properly, the saddle, nut and frets must be in the correct location.

FIGURE 7.1 Fret-work is time consuming and expensive. (Photo by John LeVan)

The string nut usually erodes from the face (fret side) to the back. This can also cause the guitar to play out of tune.

Closely inspect the bridge for cracks, it can also be a telltale sign of a broken brace.

FIGURE 7.2A,B Closely examine the bridge for any separations or lifting. This problem can be deceiving, so using a small piece of copy paper will reveal any lifting or bridge separations. If you can slide the paper under the bridge, then you know it must be removed and reglued properly. (Photo by John LeVan)

You can usually tell if a top brace is loose by looking for a ripple or crease in the top.

To check the back braces, gently press on the back along the brace and listen for a creaking noise or a popping sound.

If your guitar will not stay in tune, it could be the way it is strung. Also check the bridge and neck joints for any separations.

Loose or slipping tuning keys will cause serious tuning problems. Inspect your tuners for cracks, loose gears and cracked buttons.

FIGURE 7.3 A poorly strung guitar will not stay in tune. Make sure you follow the proper procedure when restringing your guitar. (Photo by John LeVan)

A low neck angle is easily identified because the guitar will have high action even if the bridge and saddle are as low as they can go.

A high neck angle is easily identified because the guitar will have low action and a very tall saddle.

FIGURE 7.4A,B Inspect the tuning key rollers and buttons carefully. Cracks are commonly found in both and will cause tuning problems and even premature string breakage. (Photo by John LeVan)

FIGURE 7.5 If the fret-end is sharp, the guitar dried out and needs to be humidified. (Photo by John LeVan)

Figure 7.6 Body cracks can be deceiving, use as much natural light as possible when you inspect the body. (Photo by John LeVan)

With the information discussed in the previous chapters of this book, you should be able to identify each of these problems by thoroughly inspecting the instrument you are considering. Many of these ailments are very expensive to repair, so be very attentive and meticulous when you conduct your inspection.

Other Upgrades and Repairs

There are several ways to upgrade and improve your guitar's performance without detracting from its value. Below are a few examples of how to upgrade your instrument.

Installing a Strap Button

Most classical guitars do not have a strap button because they are played while the player is sitting. If you feel that you would like a strap button on your classical guitar, here is the procedure.

List of Components

- Neck
- Heel
- Strap Button
- Button Screw
- Felt Washer
- 3/32" Drill Bit
- Drill
- Medium-Tip Phillips Head Screwdriver
- Large-Tip Phillips Head Screwdriver

The installation of a strap button is a relatively easy project, as long as you follow a few basic steps.

1. Determine the best location to install the strap button.
2. Mark the location of the screw.
3. Pre-drill the screw hole for the strap button.
4. Gently countersink the finish around the screw hole using the medium- and then the large-tip Phillips-head screwdriver.
5. Push screw through the strap button and add the felt washer at the end.
6. Screw the strap button screw into the heel with a screwdriver.

FIGURE 8.1 Location is everything. I recommend installing the button 1" below the fretboard on the treble side of the neck. If the button is installed too low on the heel, the guitar will tilt away from you when you use your guitar strap. If you place the button too high, your hand will bump it when you play on the higher frets. Once you have determined the proper location to install the strap button, gently mark it with a medium-tip Phillips-head screwdriver. Be careful not to slip and scratch the heel. (Photo by John LeVan)

FIGURE 8.2 Using a 3/32" drill bit, drill a hole into the heel to the depth of the screw only. It is also important to drill the hole at the correct angle as the screw, perpendicular to the heel. (Photo by John LeVan)

FIGURE 8.3 Using your medium-tip phillips head screwdriver, spin the handle while gently countersinking the finish around the hole. Then use a large tip phillips head screwdriver. Don't bore into the wood too far, you only need to countersink the finish enough for the screw to clear it. This will prevent any finish from peeling up when you install the screw. (Photo by John LeVan)

FIGURE 8.4 Insert the screw into the strap button and add the felt washer to the end of the screw. Screw the strap button screw into the heel and you are finished. Make sure that you don't over-tighten the screw. It can strip the wood if you torque the screw too much. (Photo by John LeVan)

Tuning Keys

List of Components

- Headstock
- Tuning Keys
- Mounting Screws
- Tuning Key Hole
- Tuning Key Button
- Tuning Key Roller

The quality of your tuning keys will make a big difference in respect to your guitar's ability to stay in tune. The higher the turning ratio, the better it will tune. In other words, the more times you have to turn the button to achieve one revolution of the tuning key roller, the finer the tuning. The turning ratio of most tuning keys will range from 11:1 to 18:1. For example, 11:1 to 14:1 is a terrible turning ratio, 15:1 up to 16:1 is a good turning ratio, and 18:1 and up is an excellent turning ratio.

Matching the correct tuning key to your guitar is important. There are many different types of keys on the market. Whether your guitar has a set of vintage keys or the latest locking keys, chances are you will find a set that will be an exact retrofit for your guitar. I recommend that you only use keys that are an exact retrofit so that you don't have to alter the guitar to install them. Altering a guitar to replace the keys will adversely affect it's value. Brands like Gotoh®, Hipshot® and Schaller® offer a wide range of tuning keys with good to excellent turning ratios and affordable prices. They range in price from $35 up to $125.

Tuning Key Installation

There are a few basic tools needed to replace tuning keys.

Tool List

- Small Tip Phillips-Head Screwdriver.

FIGURE 8.5 Small Phillips-head tip along with your cordless drill is perfect to remove the tuning key screws that hold the keys to the headstock. (Photo by John LeVan)

Here are the simple steps for removing the tuning keys.

1. Remove the strings from the guitar.
2. Remove the screws holding the tuning keys to the headstock.
3. Slide the tuning keys out of the headstock.

When removing the screws from the tuning keys (on the backside of the head-stock), be careful not to strip them. You may want to set your cordless drill on a slower setting.

FIGURE 8.6A,B The tuning keys should slide right out of the peg-holes in the headstock. (Photo by John LeVan)

When installing new tuning keys, be sure that they match up with the original equipment you have just removed. If the new keys don't fit into the original peg-holes, don't force them. You may not have the right keys.

FIGURE 8.7 When installing new tuning keys, never over-tourque a screw. This can easily strip out the hole and/or the screw head. There is no reason to torque it down with excessive force. (Photo by John LeVan)

After installing the new tuning keys, re-string the guitar and you're in business. The most important points are:

- Use keys that are an exact retrofit.
- Always use the correct tool for the job.
- Never over-torque a screw.

Bone String Nut

A bone string nut will improve sustain and tone of almost any guitar. Carving one isn't easy. It requires a lot of practice and patience. Here is what you need to get started

Tool and Materials List

- 100-Grit Sandpaper
- 220-Grit Sandpaper
- 1500-Grit Sandpaper
- Flat Surface
- Nut File Set
- Needle File Set
- Mechanical Pencil
- Thin Superglue®
- Superglue® Accelerator
- Q-Tips®
- Magnifying Lamp
- Scale (rule).
- Fretting Hammer.
- Flat-Head Screwdriver.
- Bone Blank.

Before you start, make sure that you have a good piece of bone to start with. If it is porous, cracked or too oily, you may have problems with it functioning properly as a string nut. Here are step-by-step instructions on carving a new string nut.

1. Remove the old nut (see Chapter 5) with a flathead screwdriver and a fretting hammer.
2. Clean out the nut slot (see Chapter 5) using your needle files.

3. Sand the nut blank to the proper width. Use the 100-grit paper to remove a lot of material and the 220-grit paper to remove just a little. The 1500-grit paper is to polish the nut blank. Make sure that the blank fits squarely into the slot, without any gaps. The blank should fit the slot snugly.

4. Mark the edges of the nut blank with your mechanical pencil to show how much material you need to remove to make it flush with the sides of the fret-board.

5. Sand one side of the nut blank, first with 220-grit, then with 1500-grit sandpaper until it is flush with the fretboard.

6. Repeat Step 5 on the other side of the nut blank.

7. Lay your scale (rule) flat on top of the frets with the edge against the face of the nut blank. Mark the blank with your pencil along the scale from the treble side to the bass side of the blank. This is your guide to keep you from carving into the nut too far. (See Figure 8.10)

8. Remove the nut blank and sand the top of it down to the pencil line (you may want to leave a little extra material on the bass side). Shape the top of the blank so that it slopes (angles) towards the headstock

9. Using your magnifying lamp, pencil and your scale (rule), measure out the string spacing on the nut blank. Generally, the two E strings are 1/8" from the edge of the fret-board. Be sure to measure from the outside of the string, not the center of the string. The rest of the strings are generally 1/4" apart (give or take 1/64"). Classical as well as some steel-stringed guitars have wider string spacing. Make sure that you measure the spacing of the strings on the old nut to get an idea of what the spacing should be for the new one. Next mark the location of each string slot on the nut blank with your pencil to the actual width of that string. The object of this exercise is to place each string the same distance from the other, **[based on the outside of the string, not the center]**

10. Cut the string slots (shallow); now is a good time to install the strings and tune them to pitch.

11. Measure the distance from the edge of the fretboard to the E strings as well as the distance between the strings. Adjust them accordingly and finish cutting the string slots to the proper depth.

12. Remove the strings, secure the nut with a drop of Super Glue® (to the face of the nut), and polish with 1,500 grit sandpaper and a polishing cloth.

13. Restring.

FIGURE 8.8 Make sure the nut blank fits in the slot, square and flush. (Photo by John LeVan)

FIGURE 8.9A,B Mark the edge of the blank and adjust it's width one side at a time. (Photo by John LeVan)

FIGURE 8.10 To measure the height of the nut, lay your scale on top of the frets and mark the face of the nut with a pencil. (Photo by John LeVan)

FIGURE 8.11 Sand the excess material off of the top of the nut blank and reshape. (Photo by John LeVan)

FIGURE 8.12 Measure to proper distance between each string in relation to the fretboard as well as string to string. (Photo by John LeVan)

FIGURE 8.13 Carve shallow slots into the nut blank and restring. (Photo by John LeVan)

FIGURE 8.14 Shore up the distances of the slots and cut them to the proper depth and distance. (Photo by John LeVan)

Polish the string nut.

Compensated Bone Saddle

A compensated bone saddle will also improve the volume, sustain and tone of most fine acoustic guitars. "Compensated" simply means that the saddle is intonated or adjusted in order to play more in tune. As with a string nut, choose a good bone blank before you start.

Tool and Materials List

- 100-Grit Sandpaper.
- 220-Grit Sandpaper.
- 1500-Grit Sandpaper.
- Flat Surface.
- Needle File Set.
- Mechanical Pencil.
- Scale (rule).
- Bone Blank.

Here are step-by-step instructions on carving a compensated bone saddle.

1. Remove the old saddle. If the old saddle fit the saddle slot well, use it for a template.

2. Place the old saddle against the new saddle blank on a flat surface. Trace the outline of the old saddle on the new saddle with your pencil.

3. Sand the new blank to match the old saddle's width, height, and radius.

4. Place the new saddle blank into the saddle slot and begin carving the top of the saddle to match the angle of each string. Make sure that you pay close attention to the intonation.

5. Polish the saddle with 1,500 grit sandpaper and a polishing cloth.

6. Restring.

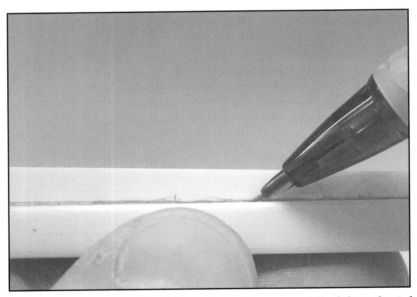

FIGURE 8.15 Use your old saddle to trace the new saddle (Photo by John LeVan)

FIGURE 8.16 Sand the new blank to proper size. (Photo by John LeVan)

FIGURE 8.17 Carve the angles for each string and intonate. (Photo by John LeVan)

Polish the saddle using 1,500 grit sandpaper. Your new bone saddle should be smooth and clean.

Other Training Resources

There are several sources of training available to aspiring luthiers. Apprenticeships, factory training and workshops are three of the best ways I know to learn and develop old and new skills. I have been fortunate to have experienced all three through other repair techs, luthiers, luthier guilds and manufacturers. I recommend these resources to anyone who wants to learn more about this ancient and fascinating trade.

Apprenticeships

The ancient tradition of apprenticeship is still alive and a great way to learn a skill or trade. An apprenticeship begins with the basics; sweeping floors, polishing guitars and taking out the trash. Eventually, you get to watch the master practice his or her craft and ask a few questions. It is best to keep a journal during your apprenticeship. There are always new questions and more profound answers. The more you learn, the more there is to know. Before you know it, you're in the middle of a neck reset or a bridge re-glue on a vintage guitar. An apprenticeship will cost you a lot of time, but it is worth it. You get back what you invest, so invest wisely.

Factory Training

For me, factory training was like working in an emergency room. I was amazed at how fast and accurate these guys worked. I thought I was efficient until I spent some time with the repair techs at the Taylor Guitar® factory. It was a crash course in everything from top replacement to bridge re-glues to neck resets. It was an amazing adventure. Factory training is one of the best ways to learn hardcore repair skills.

Workshops

When I was in Northern California, I was a part of a luthiers guild. We organized workshops and training seminars as well as swap meets. It was a great way to co-op with other luthiers to buy parts, tools and materials at a volume discount. There was always something to teach, learn and rediscover for me at the guild meetings. This is a great way to network with other luthiers to help carry on this great craft.

Glossary

0000 Steel Wool, long, hair-like threads of steel, used for cleaning, polishing and smoothing. 0000 (ultra fine) refers to the grit or cut of the steel wool.

Action, movement of parts or mechanisms. In reference to the guitar, the playability of, and/or the height of the strings in relationship to the fretboard.

Action Gauge®, tool engineered to measure the action of the guitar.

Apprenticeship, period of training, study of a craft.

Attack, velocity of strike; amount of force used to make a sound.

Binding, the wrap or gird around the body and/or neck of an instrument.

Braces, truss-like supports used to re-enforce the top and back of an an acoustic instrument.

Bridge, mechanical or stationary base that holds the strings of a guitar.

Conditioning, saturation and treatment of wood.

Crown, top or peak of a fret.

Cutaway, an area of the upper bout on the treble side of a guitar that has been removed or cutaway to give the player easier access to the higher notes on the neck.

Cyanoacrylite, transparent, thermoplastic resin containing cyanogens. Superglue®.

Cyanoacrylite Accelerator, sprayable liquid that accelerates the drying of superglue®.

Cyanoacrylite Solvent, acetone based liquid that removes superglue®.

Drift, settling or variance of a note shortly after it is struck.

Flat, 1. Level on top. 2.Lower than the ideal or desired pitch; opposite of sharp.

Fret, metal composite wire containing zinc, silver and nickel; shaped like a semicircle with a barbed stem.

Fret Guard, plastic or cardboard guard shaped like a fretboardand placed between frets and strings to prevent the strings from damaging the frets during transport.

Fret Work, the forging, shaping and polishing of frets. Includes installation, leveling, re-crowning, and burnishing.

Fretboard, slab of material, usually wood, that contains frets.

Guitar Tuner, pitch or electronic reference device used to tune a guitar.

Harmonic, generated tone whose rate of vibration is a precise multiple of that of a given fundamental tone.

Headstock, end of a neck containing the tuning keys and nut where the strings terminate.

Humidifier, a devise or machine that replaces moisture in an object or room.

Humidity, the amount of moisture in the air.

Hygrometer, gauge used to measure humidity.

Intonation, in unison, two notes matching in harmonic and fundamental pitch.

Luthier, one who builds and repairs stringed instruments.

Luthiers Guild, a group of luthiers that meets for the betterment of their craft.

Magnifying Lamp, lamp containing a magnifying lens.

Maintenance, care, upkeep and support.

Micrometer, an instrument for measuring very small distances extremely accurately.

Miniature Needle File, single cut, carbide miniature file used for various repair projects on a guitar.

Neck Angle, the degree of angle the neck has in relationship to the bridge and top of a guitar.

Nut File, carbide, double-edged files available in various width, for cutting string slots into a nut.

Partial Re-fret, replacing some but not all of the frets.

Precision Scale, 6" metal ruler used to measure in very small increments.

Radius, the circular area or distance limited by the sweep of such line. The circular arch of a fretboard, bridge saddle or string nut.

Re-crowning, to re-shape or reform the top and sides of a fret to its original shape.

Re-Fret, total replacement of frets.

Relief, the degree of forebow or backbow in a neck.

Rule of 18, equation that determines string nut and fret placement: Scale/17.817 = distance from the nut to the first fret.

Sharp, above the desired pitch, opposite of flat.

Straight Edge, metal flat stock milled extremely flat and used to gauge the forebow or backbow in a neck.

String Angle, the angle of a string in relationship to its beginning and termination.

String Nut, bridge-like, slotted object that holds the strings in place at the head-stock.

String Slots, channels cut at various depths and widths in the string nut.

String Spacing, the distance between each string slot.

String Winder, a device used to rapidly spin a tuning key button in order to speed up the process of re-stringing a guitar.

Temperament, varying degrees of tuning each string of an instrument to produce a more pleasant sound when multiple strings are played at the same time.

Trussrod, metal rod inside the neck of a guitar used to stabilize it.

Trussrod Nut, used to adjust the relief in a neck.

Tuning Key, mechanical device used to tighten or loose guitar strings.

Variable, something that is likely to change.

Velocity, swiftness or speed of motion.

Wood Glue, water-based resin.

X-Acto® Knife, small sharp knife with a pencil-like handle.